# GET IN THE KITCHEN
## Bit@hes!
### this ain't your grandma's cookbook

## by jason bailin

# WHAT'S IN IT FOR YOU,
## Bit@h?

# READ THIS *Bit@h!*

## *...and don't let me find out that you skipped it!*

I know that most of you probably don't read the acknowledgement section of a book. Unfortunately, in this particular case, you have no choice. There have been many people who have helped mold the masterpiece that is me, and damn it, you're gonna sit there and read about them.

This book is dedicated to my main bitches: My mother Helen, for passing on to me her intelligence and a strong and feisty personality. You have shaped me in more ways than you may realize and made me into the bitch I am today. I truly thank you; My father Larry, for teaching me to not be afraid to take risks, and go out on my own if necessary. Without your lead, guidance, and support, I would certainly not have had the courage to follow my heart in this endeavor; My brothers David and Andrew, for simultaneously beating and building me up. Without your tough love and encouragement, I would not be the person I have become (and by the way, I have become someone pretty damn awesome); My sister-in-law Melissa, for your love and giving me the most precious nephew, Logan, whom without, I would not be inspired to create.

4

This book is also dedicated to the memories of Grandma Lilly, and Grandpa's Charlie, and Willie. I see so much of you in me. And lastly. To my grandmother Florence, whose logic, intelligence and uncanny ability to understand people shaped a life that I aspire to emulate. Not to mention, her amazing culinary skills. You will be so dearly missed.

To my friends and models, Mona Simon, Kristin Crane, Adam Nirenberg, Daris Frencha, Christine B. and Justina Banks. You helped my words come alive with the selfless act of letting me dress you up and flaunt your sexy bodies. For allowing my book to become the best it can be, I am forever in your debt.

Thanks to my good friends for all of your support, candor and most importantly your trust! Thanks also to their husbands, wives, dates, partners, and bitches for allowing yourselves to be bent over, whipped, and force fed.

Thank you very much to Sarita Dandamudi and the amazing team at Studio Snaidero Chicago, Luxe Home, Merchandise Mart for allowing us to use their beautiful showroom for the pictures, and to Kari Skaflen for capturing that beauty (and ours) on film!

RECIPE TESTERS AND GOOD *Friends*:

David and Melissa Bailin, Maciej Kostecki, Holly Amatangelo, Harisha Koneru, Mona Simon, Kristin Crane, Tammy G., Daris Frencha, Irene and Matt Sacks, Patricia and Kelly McKinell, Suzanne Cullinane and Augie Rojas, Leslie Hudson, David Jaras, Esther Park and Ryan Tagal, Lindsay and Emmet McCann, Christine B.

Ok. That certainly was one of my weaker moments. Enough of the pleasantries. For the rest of our journey  together, expect nothing less than my utmost candor, disrespect, and domination. TURN THE PAGE BITCHES AND DON'T YOU DARE LOOK *back!*

Laugh it up now bit@hes..things aren't gonna be so funny soon...

# LEGAL CRAP!

## *...especially for you money hungry bit@hes.*

As a result of this country's love for litigation, my lawyers and I thought it would be best if we addressed some legal issues up front.

Let it be known: If in the course of reading this book and testing out any of the recipes, you, in any way suffer physical, emotional, or any other type of injury known or not known to the human race, Whipped & Beaten Culinary Works, Inc. and this book's author assume no liability.

If you in any way utilize this book for purposes it was not intended such as:

- trying to have sex with it;
- deciding to shove it up your spouse's, partner's, or anyone else's ass;
- utilizing any of the pages to clean up bodily excrement;

Whipped & Beaten Culinary Works, Inc. and this book's author again, assume no liability. No liability at all. I mean it. Seriously. None.

If you attempt a recipe and screw it up, it is all your damn fault. This includes but is not limited to:

- under or overcooking any product mentioned;
- incurring any injury in the process of reading about, preparing, or consuming the meals. Including, but not limited to:
  - burns incurred during preparation;
  - lacerations incurred while preparing the food;
  - burns incurred from your spouse or partner spreading hot, prepared food on your body or vice versa;
  - lacerations incurred while stabbing someone or getting stabbed on or near the book;
  - suffering a heart attack while having sex on or near the book;
  - incurring a paper cut while turning a page.

In short, you are on your own now that I have your money. If you choose to continue reading this book and subsequently to try a recipe, do so AT YOUR OWN DAMN RISK!

Also, don't you dare let me catch you using any part of the book without the express written consent of the publisher, the author, or Whipped & Beaten Culinary Works, Inc. As all material is protected by copyright laws, you will be severely punished by the full extent of the law...and by me.

# WARNING: *Politically Incorrect Material Enclosed!*

I am an honest person. I am also mean. Therefore, you may not like everything you are about to read. If you are offended by anything written on these pages—tough damn sh*t. It is not my responsibility to censor your reading material and therefore, Whipped & Beaten Culinary Works, Inc. and myself again, assume no liability, legal or otherwise. My professional advice: get over it.

Nuff Said.

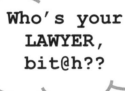

Who's your
LAWYER,
bit@h??

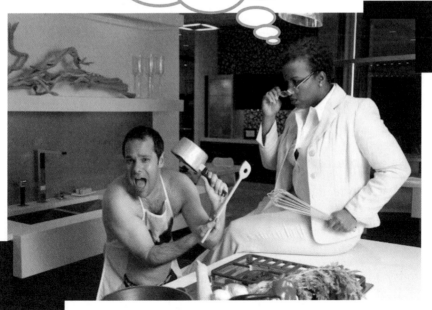

# ASSUME THE
## *Position!*

It's been a long day. You just got home from work. All you want to
do is sit back, have a glass of wine, a scotch, or a beer and plop
down in front of the TV to watch "The Apprentice gets Married to
the Bachelorette, hosted by the cast of Desperate Housewives." Oh
yeah, and eat something. Damn! "I'm too tired to cook. Why don't I
just order in?" you ask yourself. Great idea! Load yourself up with
greasy pizza, high calorie Chinese food, or whatever other ass-adding,
gut-building crap you usually inhale. But hey, it's quick and easy.
Let's face it you fat, lazy slob...you're not doing yourself any favors
by stuffing your huge mouth with sh*tty food. Here's an idea: Quit
your damn whining and GET IN THE KITCHEN, BITCH!

Listen people, I am not a chef. In fact, I spend most of my
day in an office researching stocks and bonds. Yes, of course I
have a sense of what foods go together and good ideas of
how to "spice things up." After you read this book and try some
of the recipes, you will too. It is my hope that this book will
take you from the lowly, pathetic, piece of crap cook you are
today to one that can prepare a meal simply by feeling your
way through it. It is the aim of this book to train and

discipline you, so that you not only act like a cook, but can actually be one.

Your goal should not be to simply memorize these recipes, but to understand why they taste good and to gain a sense of what foods work well together. To that end, after each recipe I will point out a few tips aimed at teaching you why the dish worked. Once you get the hang of what foods and flavors taste great together, and learn a couple of cooking techniques, you will be able to create your own, amazing meals. I know that I may be hoping for too much from a sub-par person like yourself, and that I am probably over-estimating your capabilities, but I think you can prove me wrong, bitch!

O.K., let's get back to you and your fat ass. If you haven't noticed yet, this cookbook is slightly different than what you may be used to. First of all, I am not going to coddle you, or hold your hand, or even pretend I like you. Remember, I ain't your mommy, sweetheart. I 'm your daddy, bitch. Secondly, I have designed this cookbook differently from other conventional books. Turn the page to see how.

1.  Each recipe in this book is designed for you, whether you are single, living with someone in sin, partnered or married. The recipes are designed for one or two people with enough for leftovers tomorrow.
2.  Secondly, under each recipe you will see the "Sides and More" (S&M) section where I list appetizers, salads, and sides that would work great with what you have chosen to make for an entrée. That way it isn't so hard to create a full meal, even if it's just for your own lonely, pitiful self.
3.  And finally, each recipe is labeled according to three levels of difficulty so that you know exactly what you're getting yourself into. Here's how it works:

# INGENIOUS RATING *System!*

## DUMB *Ass!*

These are meant for the culinary challenged. Even you can make these meals, dumb ass.

## THE LITTLE CHEF THAT *Could!*

I think you can, I think you can.

## ARE YOU F%@KING KIDDING *Me?*

These might take a little extra time—and a brain. While these recipes are definitely a challenge, they can be mastered by all. Don't be a wimpy piece of trash, try one.

As a result of this ground-breaking system, even someone as feeble as you will have a chance, however small, to become a good cook. By cooking your own food, you will be able to cut down on the calories that have made your ass and gut look like they do today. Plus, you're going to save so much freaking money.

# GETTING DOWN AND *Dirty!*

Ok, bitches…enough of this sweet talk. It's time to get down and dirty. Before you can cook, we need to discuss a few things. I want to train you to be good chefs, as well as good shoppers. So, the next two chapters will go through what you should have in your house at all times and will give you tips on how to shop for the food you'll need.

The first and most important thing you need when preparing to cook is…food. I know this sounds pretty self-explanatory, but I bet you have come home plenty of times, looked around the kitchen and had no substantial food to cook. Maybe you had a can of soup. Maybe a 12 year old can of refried beans. Well bitch, that sh*t just ain't gonna cut it. Is it any wonder that you spend half your salary eating out? Don't be a stupid bitch anymore. Go out and get the essentials.

Next time you go to the supermarket, make sure you pick up all of the following items. Better yet, why don't you get off your ass and go now. I know you have time, you're sitting there reading for f%@k's sake! Don't forget to take this book with you, show it to everyone you pass, and tell them how amazing it is. Also, you better not forget to tell them where they can get a copy.

This is what you are going to need:

## SPICING IT *Up!*

Every cook needs to have spices. A cook without spices is like a dominatrix without a whip. The absolute essentials are listed below. If you have these basic spices, you can make anything.

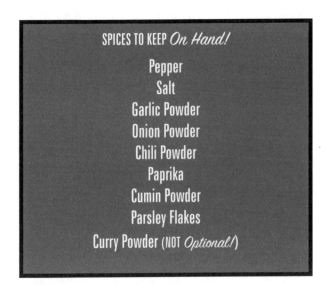

SPICES TO KEEP *On Hand!*

Pepper

Salt

Garlic Powder

Onion Powder

Chili Powder

Paprika

Cumin Powder

Parsley Flakes

Curry Powder (NOT *Optional!*)

## DON'T PLAY WITH YOUR *Meat!*

*(if you're a vegetarian skip to the next section, wus.)*

Frozen Chicken Breasts: You should always have chicken breasts in the freezer. You can make anything with chicken. They don't say "it tastes like chicken" because it was the first animal that came to mind. Also, keep other meats in the freezer so you'll have a variety on hand. Beef and pork freeze well, and are very versatile. I love using pork and beef in soups, stir fry, and pastas. There are endless possibilities.

### EAT YOUR VEGETABLES! *Or No Dessert For You!*

Fresh vegetables are obviously preferred. But who has time to ensure that there are always fresh vegetables in the house? If you can't use fresh, use frozen. If you like to use canned instead of frozen, you're an idiot. Frozen veggies are picked at the peak of their freshness and then flash frozen to retain more flavor and nutrients. Canned vegetables simply suck.

FROZEN VEGGIES TO KEEP on Hand

Corn
Broccoli
Spinach
Peas
Peas and Carrots
Cut Green Beans
Cauliflower
Zucchini

## PASTA *and Rice*

You should have three boxes of pasta and one box of packaged rice at all times. If you don't have this then go out and get some, damn it! Don't make me bend you over. Here's what I use most...hence, you should too.

---

**PASTAS AND RICE TO KEEP** *on Hand*

Penne
Mostaccioli or Ziti
Rigatoni
Farfale
Spaghetti, Linguine or Fettuccini
Ramen Noodles- They're only 25 cents a package you cheap bitch!
Rice - you should always have a box of Rice-a— Foni.

---

## SAUCY BABY, *Saucy!*

The following is a list of condiments and sauces that you should have in your home at all time. If you begin to run low on them, get your ass to the store and stock up.

**CONDIMENTS TO KEEP** *on Hand*

*Vinegar*
*Olive Oil*
*Ketchup*
*Soy Sauce*
*Hot Pepper Sauce*
*Horseradish or Dijon Mustard*

Now that I have helped you to understand what you should have in your pantry, the next step is to actually buy these necessities. I have found so many ways to save and maximize my money when I'm at the grocery store. In the next chapter I am going to pass this wisdom on to you, even though you don't deserve it. But hey, you shelled out a couple of bucks to buy this book, so it's the least I can do.

# SAVE IT FOR YOUR MOMMA!
## Helpful tips for saving money at the market!

Listen up, bitches. You can save hundreds and hundreds of dollars a year on the foods you need and want if you just show a little restraint. The following are just a few helpful hints on how you can shop wisely. Try 'em out!

### SIGN UP FOR YOUR Supermarket Club Card!:

By doing this you can take advantage of store specials without coupons. Try only buying what is on special and you can save big. Last year I added the savings up to be over $800. Here's a hint: if the item is not on sale today, wait a week or two. Soon you will start to know what items are on sale, and how frequently, so you can plan your shopping trips better.

### TRY BUYING MEAT PRODUCTS THAT ARE ON SALE or Near Their "Sell By" Date:

These products are cheaper and are just as good as the supposedly fresh meat. Many meat products are somewhat frozen before they get to the store anyway. All you have to do is put them in the freezer. This way you will always have something to start with. You will also save tons of money…about $300 a year to be exact!

## TAKE ADVANTAGE OF THE BUY-ONE-GET-ONE-FREE *Specials!:*

If it's something you use, and it's non-perishable or if it's freezable, buy it when it's BOGOF! You can use these opportunities to get twice the amount of food for the price of one. Remember, this doesn't mean you should eat it twice as fast. PIG!

## MAKE YOUR CANNED SOUPS *Go Twice as Far:*

Buy the canned soups you like. Most grocery stores periodically have sales where you can get a can of soup for 99 cents or BOGOF. Try to stock up when this is the case. To make your soup go twice or three times as far, use them as a base for your meal. Don't just heat them up. Add more water, spices, veggies and meat. his way you can make one can of soup for four people! When you put enough stuff in them, they are a great, quick meal. See the "So, too Damn Lazy to Start from Scratch, Huh?" section of this book for some recipes that show you how to make canned soup work for you.

## BUY FROZEN PIZZAS *When They are 4 for $10:*

Buy frozen pizza when it's cheap and dress it up with a few of your own touches. It makes a quick and easy meal for when you don't want to spend an hour in the kitchen. Again, see the "So, too Damn Lazy to Start from Scratch, Huh?" section.

**BUY PACKAGED RICE** *When it's on Sale:*

There are so many different things you can do with packaged rice. You can make a full meal with one box of Rice-A-Foni and other cheap ingredients. It's all in the "So, too Damn Lazy to Start from Scratch, Huh?" section, so make sure you read it.

Now that you are prepared, I think we can take the next step. The rest of the book is filled with original recipes that I have made up over the years. Just remember, if you try a recipe, and it fails, it's all your damn fault. Don't blame me. NOW GET YOUR ASS IN THE KITCHEN, *Bit@h!*

What the heck are you smiling about bit@h!?!

# GET IN THE KITCHEN,
## *Bit@h!*

## Entrées

The following are original recipes that I have invented. Until now, I have kept them a secret and have allowed only a few select friends to attempt them. However one day I was thinking to myself "Jason, you hot stud, why not share your love of cooking with the lowly bitches of the world." The product of my hard work is this masterpiece. Be proud that you had the intelligence to buy it.

You will notice that I have put tremendous thought and used a lot of creativity to name each of the dishes. Take the time to appreciate them, damn it! If you're too lazy to go through the recipes page by page, there is a full listing at the end of the book.

# SOUTH OF MY BORDER *Pasta*

## *(Taco Pasta with Chicken, Steak, Pork or Ground Meat)*

RATING: **DUMB** *Ass!*

*Grocery List:*
Packet of Taco Seasoning
Choice of: (½ lb) ground Turkey, ground Chicken, ground Beef, cubed Chicken, cubed Steak or cubed Pork
½ can of diced Tomatoes
Rigatoni, Farfale, or Penne
½ cup of chopped Carrot
¼ Onion chopped
½ cup frozen Corn
Red Wine Vinegar
Black Olives
Garlic Powder
Onion Powder
Chili Powder
Ground Black Pepper
Parmesan Cheese

## Preparation:

In a semi-deep pan, sauté onions, tomatoes and carrots in enough olive oil to coat. Add garlic powder and pepper to taste as you are sautéing. When the onions become slightly clear (one minute or so), add 3 tbsp vinegar and sauté for 30 seconds more. Add meat and sauté with ½ tsp each of garlic powder, onion powder and chili powder and 2 more tbsp of vinegar. Sauté until meat is browned. Add 1½ cups of water, 4 tbsp vinegar and ½ packet of taco seasoning. Bring to boil and add ½ lb of pasta. Add a handful of olives. Mix, cover and let simmer for about 15-20 minutes, or until you notice that water is basically gone from pan. Add 2 more tbsp of vinegar and stir. Add corn and parmesan cheese about 1 minute before turning heat off and stir.

### ADD MORE PARMESAN CHEESE IF DESIRED
### AND SERVE IT, Bit@h!

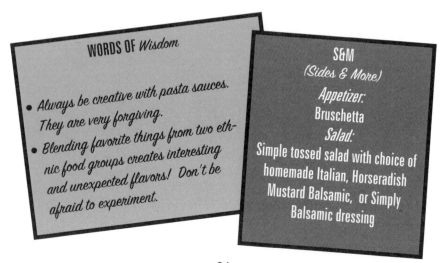

### WORDS OF Wisdom

- Always be creative with pasta sauces. They are very forgiving.
- Blending favorite things from two ethnic food groups creates interesting and unexpected flavors! Don't be afraid to experiment.

### S&M
#### (Sides & More)

*Appetizer:*
Bruschetta

*Salad:*
Simple tossed salad with choice of homemade Italian, Horseradish Mustard Balsamic, or Simply Balsamic dressing

# LICK MY BOOTS *Lamb*/BEND ME OVER *Beef*
## *(Braised Lamb or Beef in a Red Wine Onion Sauce)*

RATING: **THE LITTLE CHEF THAT** *Could*

*Grocery List*
Lamb Shank or Pot Roast
½ Onion chopped
2 Garlic cloves chopped
1 packet of Onion Soup mix
1½ cups Red Wine
1 tbsp Worcestershire Sauce
Garlic Powder
Onion Powder
Parsley Flakes
Ground Black Pepper
Olive Oil
Butter
Flour

Anything for a Brother.

# Preparation:

## MARINADE:

Add one packet of onion soup mix to 2 cups of boiling water. Boil for 2 minutes and let cool. In a bowl combine 1½ cups of red wine, 1-2 tbsp of Worcestershire sauce, 2 tbsp of garlic powder, ½ tsp of ground black pepper, 1 tbsp of parsley flakes, and cooled onion soup.

Marinate lamb chops or beef overnight in prepared marinade, covered tightly in refrigerator.

## COOKING:

Mix ½ tbsp of pepper and enough flour to make a thin layer on a dinner plate.

Coat meat in flour mix lightly on either side.

In a coverable, semi-deep frying pan, sauté onion and garlic in enough olive oil to coat. Add a pinch of pepper to season. Add enough red wine to cover the bottom of the pan. Add three splashes of Worcestershire sauce. Evenly mix with wooden spoon on medium-high heat. Brown lamb or beef on each side for 1-2 minutes or until you see flour turn a golden color. Take out of pan and set aside.

Pour marinade into frying pan. Add 2 pats of butter. Cover and bring to a boil for thirty seconds. Then simmer over low heat. When mixture has come to a simmer put the meat into pan and cover tightly. Simmer for 2-3 hours.

GRAVY:

Remove meat from pan. Add 1 pat of butter to leftover sauce and stir until melted. Stir in 2 tbsp of flour slowly until the sauce thickens. If it does not thicken after 3 minutes, slowly add more flour.

## PUT GRAVY ON MEAT AND SERVE IT, *Bit@h!*

### S&M
*(Sides & More)*

*Appetizer:*
Bruschetta
Baked Artichoke

*Salad:*
Simple tossed salad with choice of any homemade dressing

*Choice of Sides:*
Zesty Lemon Garlic Potatoes
Veggie Mashed Potatoes
Curry Cinnamon Mashed Sweet Potatoes
Potato, Broccoli and Cheese Kugel
Vegetable Kugel
Sweet Potato Kugel

### Words Of *Wisdom*

- Red meats are complemented by red wines.
- Onion and salty flavors de-intensify a wine's boldness.
- When using salty sauces or flavorings, there is no need to add more salt.

# ON YOUR KNEES! *Chicken*
## (Chicken with a Lemon White Wine Butter Sauce)

RATING: **ARE YOU F%@KING KIDDING** *Me?*

*Grocery List:*

2-4 Chicken Breasts
2 cloves of Garlic sliced
1 Lemon
½ Onion sliced
¼ stick of Butter
1 can of Chicken Broth
Salt
Ground Black Pepper
Parsley Flakes
White Wine
Flour
Parmesan Cheese
Garlic Powder
Onion Powder
1 Egg

**S&M**
*(Sides & More)*
*Appetizer:*
Baked Artichoke
Bruschetta
*Salad:*
Simple tossed salad with choice of
any homemade dressing
*Choice of Sides:*
Zesty Lemon Garlic Potatoes Broccoli
and Garlic in Lemon Butter

**WORDS OF** *Wisdom*
- *White wine sauces allow chicken to have a lighter flavor.*
- *Lemon and garlic together lightens up the flavor of White wine.*
- *Adding citrus to White wine tames the wine's flavor and brings out its essence.*

## Preparation:

Mix ½ cup flour with 2 tbsp parmesan cheese, 1 tsp garlic powder, 1 tsp onion powder, 1 tsp parsley flakes, ½ tsp of pepper and a pinch of salt. Crack 1 egg in separate bowl and beat with 1 tsp parmesan cheese, 1 tsp parsley flakes, pinch of pepper and a pinch of salt. Prepare chicken pieces by covering in flour mixture, then egg mixture and then dredging in flour mixture again. Set aside.

In a semi-deep, coverable frying pan, sauté onion and garlic with enough olive oil to coat. Add pinch of garlic powder, salt and pepper. Sauté for 1 minute. Add enough white wine to cover bottom of pan and juice of ½ lemon. Brown chicken on either side for 30 seconds to one minute until flour mixture is cooked through and adheres to chicken. Take out and set aside.

In same pan, add chicken broth, ¼ cup white wine, ¼ stick of butter, 1 tbsp of garlic powder, juice of ½ lemon, 1 tbsp of onion powder, 1 tbsp parsley flakes, ½ tsp of pepper, salt to taste. Bring to a boil, then simmer. Add chicken (only when it has stopped boiling, no sooner.) Cover and simmer for 45 minutes.

Take chicken out and set aside. Using the sauce mixture slowly stir in 2 tbsp of flour to thicken. Stir until fairly smooth, try to get all lumps out.

### DISH OUT SAUCE OVER CHICKEN, MAKING SURE TO INCLUDE SOME ONIONS AND GARLIC, AND SERVE IT, *Bit@h!*

# THE SAUCY *Russian*

## *(Pasta with Creamy Vodka Tomato Bolognese)*

RATING: **THE LITTLE CHEF THAT** *Could*

*Grocery List:*

Choice of ground Chicken, Turkey or Beef
Olive Oil
2 cloves of Garlic chopped or sliced
½ Onion chopped
1 can of Tomato Paste
Juice of ½ Lemon
½ cup Vodka
½ cup of Half and Half or Heavy Cream
½ cup frozen Peas
3 tbsp Parmesan Cheese
Parsley Flakes
Ground Black Pepper
Salt
Penne, Rigatoni, or Mostaccioli

You'll be pretty yet, bit@h!

30

## Preparation:

In a coverable, semi-deep frying pan, sauté onion and garlic in enough olive oil to coat. Add a pinch of salt and pepper. Sauté ground meet with onion and garlic for approximately 1½ minutes until it starts to brown. Add the tomato paste and stir until it is consistent and smooth. Add salt and pepper to taste. Add juice of ½ lemon. Over medium heat, add the vodka and cream and stir until sauce is consistent in color and texture. Cover and simmer for 45 minutes, stirring occasionally to make sure sauce doesn't stick to bottom of pan.

Prepare pasta as indicated on box. Two minutes prior to serving, add the pasta and parmesan cheese to sauce and fully coat. One minute prior to serving, add frozen peas. Stir and make sure all peas have been defrosted and are bright green.

### ADD PARMESAN TO TASTE AND
### SERVE IT, *Bit@h!*

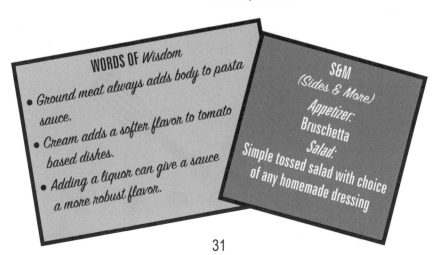

WORDS OF *Wisdom*
- Ground meat always adds body to pasta sauce.
- Cream adds a softer flavor to tomato based dishes.
- Adding a liquor can give a sauce a more robust flavor.

S&M
(Sides & More)
Appetizer:
Bruschetta
Salad:
Simple tossed salad with choice of any homemade dressing

# THE SPECIAL SAUCY *Russian*

## *(The Saucy Russian with Chunks of Beef, Veal and Pork)*

RATING: **THE LITTLE CHEF THAT** *Could*

*Grocery List:*
Olive Oil
1 lb (all together) Veal, Beef and Pork cubed
1 can of Tomato Paste
2 cloves of Garlic chopped or sliced
1/3 Onion chopped
Juice of ½ Lemon
½ cup Vodka
½ cup of Half and Half or Heavy Cream
½ cup frozen Peas
3 tbsp Parmesan Cheese
Parsley Flakes
Ground Black Pepper
Salt
Penne, Rigatoni, Mostaccioli

## Preparation:

In a coverable, semi-deep frying pan, sauté onion and garlic in enough olive oil to coat. Add a pinch of salt and pepper. Sauté veal, beef and pork with onion and garlic for approximately 1½ minutes until it starts to brown. Add the tomato paste and stir until it is consistent and smooth. Add salt and pepper to taste. Add juice of ½ lemon. Over medium heat, add the vodka and cream and stir until sauce is consistent in color and texture. Cover and simmer for 45 minutes, stirring occasionally to make sure sauce doesn't stick to bottom of pan.

Prepare pasta as indicated on box. Two minutes prior to serving, add the pasta and parmesan cheese to sauce and fully coat. One minute prior to serving, add frozen peas. Stir and make sure all peas have been defrosted and are bright green.

### ADD PARMESAN TO TASTE AND SERVE IT, *Bit@h!*

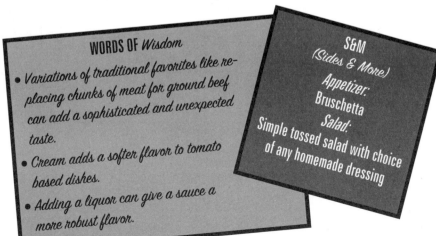

WORDS OF *Wisdom*
- *Variations of traditional favorites like replacing chunks of meat for ground beef can add a sophisticated and unexpected taste.*
- *Cream adds a softer flavor to tomato based dishes.*
- *Adding a liquor can give a sauce a more robust flavor.*

S&M
(*Sides & More*)
*Appetizer:*
Bruschetta
*Salad:*
Simple tossed salad with choice of any homemade dressing

# BOMBAY *Booty*
## (Beer Soaked Chicken Curry)

RATING: **DUMB** *Ass!*

This recipe can be great for Kebabs or Barbecue!

*Grocery List:*
2-4 Chicken Breasts (cubed if for kebabs)
1 can of Beer
Curry Powder
Garlic Powder
Salt
Ground Black Pepper
Chili Powder
Onion Powder
Paprika
1 Lime
1 Onion sliced (fajita style)
1 clove Garlic
1 Green Pepper sliced (fajita style)
Tomatoes chopped thick
¼ stick of melted Butter

## Preparation:

### MARINADE

Combine can of beer, 1 tbsp of curry powder, 1 tbsp chili powder, 1 tsp garlic powder, 1 tsp onion powder, 1 tsp of paprika, salt and pepper to taste, juice of 1 lime and ¼ stick of melted butter. Marinate chicken and vegetables together for at least two hours.

### COOKING *Options*

Grilling: Grill vegetables and chicken. Put on Kebab if desired.

On A Stove: Sauté sliced onions and sliced garlic cloves in enough olive oil to coat. Add vegetables and chicken and sauté until chicken is browned. Add enough marinade so that chicken and vegetables are ¼ to ½ submerged. Bring to a boil for 30 seconds and then simmer. Add a pat of butter. Stir and cover and simmer for 30 minutes.

## SERVE IT,
### *Bit@h!*

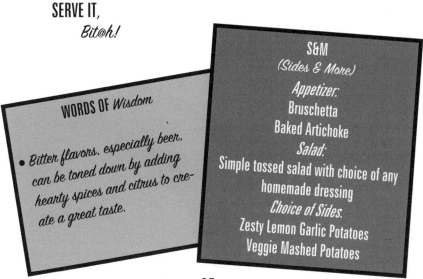

WORDS OF *Wisdom*

- *Bitter flavors, especially beer, can be toned down by adding hearty spices and citrus to create a great taste.*

S&M
*(Sides & More)*
*Appetizer:*
Bruschetta
Baked Artichoke
*Salad:*
Simple tossed salad with choice of any homemade dressing
*Choice of Sides:*
Zesty Lemon Garlic Potatoes
Veggie Mashed Potatoes

# VIJAY RODRIGUES' *Tacos*
## *(Chicken Curry Tacos)*

**RATING: THE LITTLE CHEF THAT** *Could*

*Grocery List:*
Olive Oil
2 cloves of Garlic
½ Onion
2 Tomatoes
2-4 Chicken breasts sliced
Curry Powder
Chili Powder
Fresh Cilantro
1 Lemon
Broccoli
Hot Pepper Sauce
1 Potato
Salt
Ground Black Pepper
Light Sour Cream
White Rice
Corn Tortillas
Garlic Powder

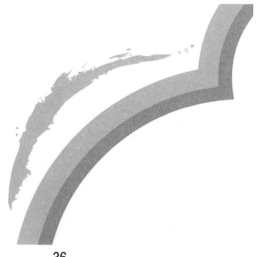

## Preparation:

In a blender combine 2 cups of light sour cream, juice of ½ lemon, ¼ onion, 1 clove of garlic, ½ tomato, ¼ cup of fresh cilantro, 1 tbsp of hot pepper sauce, 2 tbsp curry powder, 1 tsp of chili powder, salt to taste, ½ tsp of ground black pepper, 1 tbsp olive oil. Blend until smooth. Set aside.

Slice potato into chunks. Cut broccoli into bite sized pieces. Cut rest of tomatoes into chunks. Set aside.

In a large, deep, pot, sauté 1 clove of garlic chopped or sliced, ¼ onion chopped with juice of ¼ lemon and enough olive oil to coat. Sauté for 1 minute.

Add potatoes and stir frequently so they don't stick to bottom of pot for about two minutes. Add chicken and sauté until browned. Add blended mixture to pot, stir and bring to a boil. Then simmer. Add broccoli and tomato. Simmer until potatoes are tender. Stir occasionally to prevent food from burning and sticking to bottom of pot.

Prepare rice as directed.

### PREPARING *Taco*

Heat tortillas if desired. Put tortilla on the plate, followed by a layer of rice, followed by chicken and vegetable mix.

## ROLL AND SERVE IT,
### *Bit@h!*

## S&M
*(Sides & More)*

*Appetizer:*
Baked Artichoke
Bruschetta

*Salad:*
Simple tossed salad with choice of
homemade dressing

## WORDS OF *Wisdom*

- Blending favorite things from two ethnic food groups creates interesting and unexpected flavors! Don't be afraid to experiment.
- Curry is toned down and its flavor is revealed when a cream based product is added to it.
- Lemon and cilantro add a great zesty and lighter flavor to rich, cream based dishes.

That Taco
rolled tight
enough,
Bit@h!?!

38

# CURRY THE F%@K Up!

*(Easy Chicken Curry With Rice)*

RATING: **DUMB** *Ass!*

*Grocery List:*
2 Chicken Breasts cubed
Chicken Flavor packaged rice
1 clove Garlic sliced
¼ Onion chopped
½ cup frozen Broccoli
½ cup frozen Peas
1 Lemon
White Wine
Fresh Cilantro
Curry Powder
Chili Powder
Ground Black Pepper
Hot Pepper Sauce

## Preparation:

In a semi-deep, coverable frying pan, sauté onion, garlic, and cilantro in enough olive oil to coat. Add juice of ¼ lemon, ½ tsp of curry powder, ½ tsp of chili powder, hot pepper sauce and pepper to taste. Add enough white wine to cover bottom of pan. Sauté for 30 seconds to one minute. Add cubed chicken and sauté for additional minute. Add packaged rice and sauté until rice becomes semi-browned (1 additional minute or so.)

Add two cups of water and stir in 1/3 packet of chicken flavor seasoning (it is imperative not to use much more than this or the chicken flavor will take over dish). Squeeze the rest of the juice from the lemon, add 1 tsp of curry powder, ½ tsp of chili powder. Stir and bring to a boil. Bring to a simmer, then add broccoli and stir. Cover tightly and let liquid absorb into rice. One minute before serving add frozen peas and stir until defrosted and bright green.

### SCOOP INTO A BOWL AND SERVE IT,
*Bit@h!*

S&M
(Sides & More)
Appetizer:
Baked Artichoke
Bruschetta
Salad:
Simple tossed salad with choice of homemade dressing

WORDS OF *Wisdom*
• Packaged food products can provide a great starting point for easy meals (see the "So, Too Damn Lazy to Start From Scratch, Huh?" section for more details.
• Lemon adds a great, unexpected flavor to salty dishes.

# NEW DELHI *Meatloaf*
## *(Curry Meatloaf)*

RATING: **DUMB** *Ass!*

*Grocery List:*
1   Potato
¼ Onion diced
2 Garlic cloves chopped
1lb of ground Turkey or Chicken (can use beef, but I find the poultry more appealing for this dish)
½ cup frozen Peas
1 Lemon
Curry Powder
Chili Powder
1 Egg
Bread Crumbs
Salt
Ground Black Pepper
Cayenne Pepper
Olive Oil

## Preparation:

Grate the potato into thin strings in a strainer and squeeze excess water out. Place in a bowl and squeeze juice of ½ lemon and mix to keep from getting brown. In same bowl, combine ground meat, onion, garlic, peas, rest of the lemon juice, 1 tbsp of curry powder, 1 tsp of chili powder, egg, ¼ cup of bread crumbs, 1-2 tsp salt, ½ tsp ground black pepper, ½ tsp cayenne pepper if desired,  and 2 tbsp olive oil. Mix thoroughly until even.

Preheat oven to 350 degrees. Place meat mixture into greased baking pan. Bake for 45 minutes to an hour.

### CUT AND SERVE IT,
#### Bit@h!

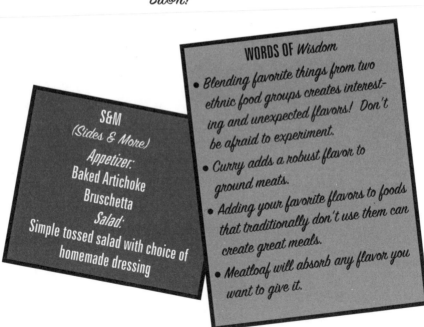

**S&M**
(Sides & More)
*Appetizer:*
Baked Artichoke
Bruschetta
*Salad:*
Simple tossed salad with choice of homemade dressing

**WORDS OF *Wisdom***

- Blending favorite things from two ethnic food groups creates interesting and unexpected flavors! Don't be afraid to experiment.
- Curry adds a robust flavor to ground meats.
- Adding your favorite flavors to foods that traditionally don't use them can create great meals.
- Meatloaf will absorb any flavor you want to give it.

# SPICY YOUNG THANG *Meatloaf*
## *(Spicy Style Meatloaf)*

RATING: **DUMB** *Ass!*

*Grocery List:*
Hot Pepper Sauce
Garlic Powder
Onion Powder
Parsley Flakes
Vinegar
Ketchup
Chili Powder
Salt
½ cup chopped Celery
2 Garlic cloves chopped
Ground Black Pepper
1 lb of ground Turkey or
Chicken (can
use beef, but I find the poultry
more appealing for this dish)
¼ Onion diced
1 Potato
1 Egg
Bread Crumbs
Olive Oil

Oi! You are a spicy young thang, bit@h!

43

## Preparation:

### SPICY Sauce

In a bowl combine ¼ cup of ketchup, 4 tbsp red wine vinegar, 2 tbsp hot pepper sauce 1 tbsp garlic powder, 1 tbsp onion powder, ½ tsp ground black pepper, 1 tbsp parsley flakes. Mix thoroughly.

### COOKING Instructions

Grate the potato into thin strings in a strainer and squeeze excess water out. Place in a bowl. In same bowl, combine ground meat, onion, garlic, 1 tsp of chili powder, egg, ½ cup of bread crumbs, 1 tsp salt, ½ tsp ground black pepper, spicy sauce (that you made above), and 1 tbsp olive oil. Mix thoroughly until even.
Preheat oven to 350 degrees. Place meat mixture into greased baking pan. Bake for 45 minutes to an hour.

## CUT AND SERVE IT WITH RANCH OR
## BLEU CHEESE DRESSING, Bit@h!

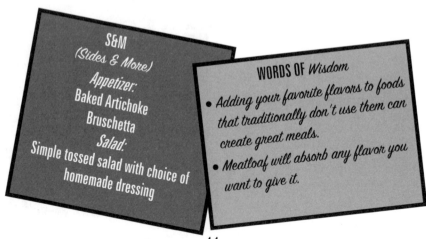

**S&M**
*(Sides & More)*
*Appetizer:*
Baked Artichoke
Bruschetta
*Salad:*
Simple tossed salad with choice of
homemade dressing

WORDS OF *Wisdom*
- Adding your favorite flavors to foods that traditionally don't use them can create great meals.
- Meatloaf will absorb any flavor you want to give it.

# LOVE YOU LONG TIME PORK *Ribs*

## *(Pork Ribs in Asian Barbecue Sauce)*

RATING: **DUMB** *Ass!*

*Grocery List:*

Hoison Sauce
Hickory BBQ Sauce
Ketchup
Vinegar
Soy Sauce
Hot Pepper Sauce
Pepper
Garlic Powder
Onion Powder
Curry Powder
Chili Powder
Honey
4-6 Pork Ribs
½ Onion sliced
2 cloves Garlic chopped
Flour

**S&M**
*(Sides & More)*

*Appetizer:*
Baked Artichoke
Bruschetta

*Salad :*
Asian Cucumber Salad

*Choice of Sides:*
Eat Me! Eggplant
Zesty Lemon Garlic Potatoes
Curry Cinnamon Mashed Sweet Potatoes
Vegetable Kugel
Sweet Potato Kugel

## *Preparation:*

### MARINADE

In a large bowl, combine ½ cup of ketchup, 3 tbsp Hoison Sauce, ¼ cup of hickory barbecue sauce, 1 tbsp of soy sauce, 2 tbsp hot pepper sauce, 2 tbsp of honey, 2 tbsp vinegar, 1 tsp chili powder, 1 tbsp of curry powder, ½ tbsp of pepper, 1 tbsp garlic powder, 1 tbsp of onion powder, 1 ½ cups of water. Mix thoroughly until even. Marinate pork ribs for 1-2 hours or overnight if you have time.

### COOKING

In a semi-deep, coverable pan, sauté onion and garlic in enough olive oil to coat for one minute. Gently brown the ribs on both sides for thirty seconds, enough to simply sear the meat. Then take out and set aside. Pour marinade into pan and bring to a boil for 30 seconds then lower heat to simmer. When sauce is simmering, place ribs into mixture. Cover and cook for 3-5 hours (depending on how tender you desire).

After 3-5 hours add 1-2 tbsp of flour and continuously stir to thicken sauce. If it doesn't turn into gravy, then add more flour. Place ribs back into gravy for one or two minutes to heat them up.

## SERVE THOSE RIBS,
### Bit@h!

> **WORDS OF *Wisdom***
> • *Altering a typical barbeque sauce can really bring unexpected and rich flavor to meats.*
> • *Blending similar flavors from different cuisines complement each other and enhance each others taste.*

# PULL MY FINGER! *Pork*
## *(Pork in a Zesty Cranberry Onion Sauce)*

**RATING: THE LITTLE CHEF THAT** *Could*

*Grocery List:*
1 packet Onion Soup Mix
3 tbsp Red Horseradish from a jar (can be found in refrigerated section of grocery store)
1 can of Whole Cranberry Sauce
Ground Black Pepper
Pork Roast
2 pats of Butter
Olive Oil

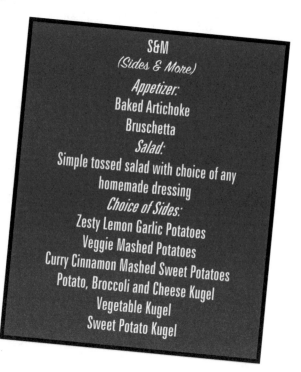

S&M
*(Sides & More)*

*Appetizer:*
Baked Artichoke
Bruschetta

*Salad:*
Simple tossed salad with choice of any homemade dressing

*Choice of Sides:*
Zesty Lemon Garlic Potatoes
Veggie Mashed Potatoes
Curry Cinnamon Mashed Sweet Potatoes
Potato, Broccoli and Cheese Kugel
Vegetable Kugel
Sweet Potato Kugel

## Preparation:

### MARINADE

In a pot, add 1 packet of onion soup mix to 2 cups of water. Over medium heat, add half can of whole cranberry sauce, 2 tbsp of red horseradish, 1 tsp of ground black pepper. Allow to cool. Pour into a large bowl and marinate pork for 1-2 hours at room temperature covered or overnight if possible covered in the refrigerator.

### COOKING

In a frying pan, combine 1 tbsp of olive oil with two pats of butter and heat. Remove pork from marinade and brown on all sides. Place pork in baking pan and pour marinade over meat. Cover with aluminum foil. Preheat oven to 350 degrees and bake for 2 hours.

### GRAVY

Pour left over juices into a semi deep frying pan and bring to a boil. Reduce heat to medium-low. Stir in 1-2 tbsp of flour slowly. Stir until gravy thickens. Add more flour if sauce does not thicken.

### WORDS OF Wisdom

- Adding salty flavors to fruity flavors will convert the sweetness from a typical desert-type dish to a dinner-type dish.
- Horseradish can add unexpected flavor and zest to tastes that don't possess them without being too powerful.
- Onion and fruit always go together.
- Pork is always complementary to a fruit based sauce.

## SLICE PORK AGAINST GRAIN,
### POUR GRAVY OVER MEAT AND SERVE IT, Bit@h!

# POKE ME! *Pork*
## *(Pork with Spiced Curry Apple Sauce)*

### RATING: ARE YOU F%@KING KIDDING *Me?*

*Grocery List:*
Pork Roast
Olive Oil
Salt
Ground Black Pepper
¼ Onion chopped
2 Garlic cloves sliced
Curry Powder
Chili Powder
Sherry Wine
1 can of Chicken Broth
Cranberry juice
Butter
Cinnamon
Garlic Powder
2 Apples
Flour

## *Preparation:*

Flour pork—press all sides in flour.

Sauté fresh garlic and onions in enough olive oil to coat until onions start to brown. Add pinch of salt and pepper. Add ¼ tsp of curry powder (enough to spread around, don't go crazy). Add ¼ tsp of chili powder.  Add enough Sherry wine to spread around bottom of pan. Heat to medium high. Brown each side of pork. Remove pork and set aside.

In same pan, add 1 cup of cranberry juice, 1 tsp curry powder, 1 tsp chili powder, 1 tsp salt, 1 tsp pepper and 1 tsp garlic powder. Add 1 cup sherry and 1 can of chicken broth with ¼ stick of butter. Bring to boil then let simmer. While simmering, add pork, cover for 2 hours.

### SAUCE:

About 15-20 minutes before pork has finished simmering, cut up apples and boil them in a pot. Mash apples in pot and set aside until pork has cooked. When pork has cooked, take out of pan and set aside. Add apples to sauce that pork was cooking in. Add 1 tsp of cinnamon and slowly stir 2 tbsp flour into sauce until sauce has thickened. If sauce does not come to a gravy-like thickness, then add more flour. Place pork back into gravy for two minutes to heat up.

### SLICE PORK AGAINST GRAIN, POUR GRAVY OVER MEAT
### AND SERVE IT, *Bit@h!*

## S&M
### (Sides & More)

*Appetizer:*
Baked Artichoke
Bruschetta

*Salad:*
Simple tossed salad with choice of any homemade dressing

*Choice of Sides:*
Curry Cinnamon Mashed Sweet Potatoes
Sweet Potato Kugel
Begg Me!

## WORDS OF *Wisdom*

• Adding salty flavors to fruity flavors will convert the sweetness from a typical desert-type dish to a dinner-type dish.

• Curry, cinnamon, and apple are complementary flavors.

• Onion and fruit always go together.

• Pork is always complementary to a fruit based sauce.

• Flour will thicken any meat juice to become gravy. Add a little butter to enhance flavor and thicken.

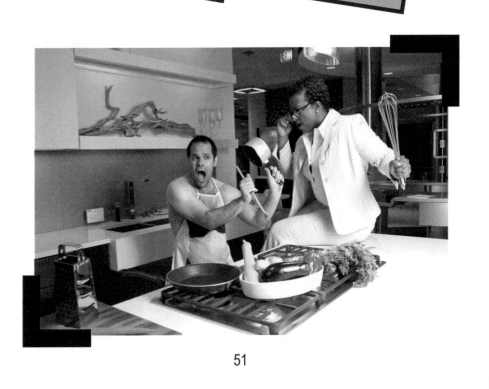

# HURT ME! *Hen*
## *(Cornish Hen in a Lime Marsala Sauce )*

RATING: **DUMB** *Ass!*

*Grocery List:*
Cornish Game Hen
Marsala Wine
2 Limes
Ground Black Pepper
Garlic Powder
Onion Powder
Olive Oil
Parmesan Cheese
Worcestershire Sauce

52

## Preparation:

### MARINADE:

In a bowl combine ¾ cup of Marsala Wine, ½ cup of chicken broth, juice of two limes, 3 tbsp of olive oil, 1 tbsp of Worcestershire Sauce, 2 tsp of garlic powder, 2 tsp of onion powder, 1 tbsp parmesan cheese, 1 tsp of black pepper. Mix thoroughly. Place the hen in the marinade for at least two hours.

### BAKING:

Place hen in baking pan, pour marinade over hen. Bake in oven for one and a half hours at 375 degrees, basting occasionally.

### GRAVY:

Take juices from baking pan and put in a sauce pan. Add 2 pats of butter and slowly add 2 tbsp of flour and stir until it thickens.

**CUT HEN IN HALF AND SERVE IT WITH A SIDE** *Bit@h!*

*Don't forget the gravy... dumbass.*

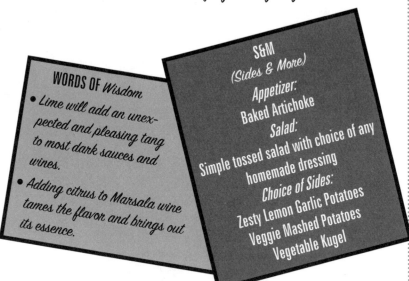

**WORDS OF** *Wisdom*

- *Lime will add an unexpected and pleasing tang to most dark sauces and wines.*
- *Adding citrus to Marsala wine tames the flavor and brings out its essence.*

**S&M**
(*Sides & More*)

Appetizer:
Baked Artichoke
Salad:
Simple tossed salad with choice of any homemade dressing
Choice of Sides:
Zesty Lemon Garlic Potatoes
Veggie Mashed Potatoes
Vegetable Kugel

# MISO HONEE STIR *Fry*

RATING: **DUMB** *Ass!*

*Grocery List:*
Soy Sauce
Balsamic Vinegar
Red Wine Vinegar
Teriyaki Sauce
Ketchup
Garlic Powder
Ground Black Pepper
Chili Powder
2 cloves of Garlic sliced
½ Onion chopped
2 Chicken Breasts
cubed
Frozen Carrots
Frozen Corn
Frozen Peas
Frozen Broccoli
Ramen Noodles

## Preparation:

### STIR FRY Sauce:

Prepare stir fry sauce by combining 1/8 cup red wine vinegar, 1/8 cup soy sauce, 1/8 cup balsamic vinegar, 1/8 cup teriyaki sauce, 1/8 cup of ketchup, 1 tsp garlic powder, 1 tsp chili powder, 1 tsp ground black pepper, 1/4 cup of water. Stir thoroughly and set aside.

### COOKING:

In a deep, coverable frying pan, sauté onion and garlic with enough olive oil to coat. Add ½ tsp of ground black pepper. Sauté for about a minute. Add diced chicken and sauté for an additional 30 seconds until chicken begins to slightly brown but it still mostly pink. Add 2 tbsp of balsamic vinegar (enough to coat meat, but not to drench it). Stir and sauté for another minute until chicken is browned. Add ½ cup each of corn, broccoli, and carrots. Add a tsp of soy sauce, ½ tsp of chili powder, ½ tsp of garlic powder, ½ tsp of ground black pepper and stir.

Add stir fry sauce and stir. Bring to a boil, cover, lower heat to medium low and simmer for a half hour. Crush Ramen Noodles in package so they are not all attached and there are small pieces. Sprinkle them in and stir so that that the noodles are coated by the sauce. Cover pan. Keep heat on low and let cook until the sauce has been absorbed into the noodles. Uncover and turn up heat to med high. Stir after sauce has been absorbed completely so that the noodles fry a bit. Turn off heat and add frozen peas. Mix until they turn bright green and are no longer frozen.

### PUT IT IN A BOWL AND
### SERVE IT Bit@h!

## WORDS OF *Wisdom*

- *Ramen noodles will work well in any Asian dish requiring pasta.*

- *Asian flavor sauces work well when toned down by the sweetness of a tomato based sauce or condiment.*

- *Vinegar and soy sauce combine to make a very flavorful dish. The acidity of vinegar is complemented by the saltiness of the soy sauce.*

### S&M
### *(Sides & More)*

*Appetizer:*
Baked Artichoke
Bruschetta

*Salad:*
Asian Cucumber Salad
Simple tossed salad with choice of homemade dressing

56

# PISTOL WHIP *Pasta*
## *(Pasta with Chicken in a Balsamic, Tomato, and Garlic Sauce)*

RATING: **THE LITTLE CHEF THAT** *Could*

*Grocery List:*

2 Chicken Breasts cubed

¼ Onion chopped

2 cloves of Garlic sliced

1 Tomato diced

Salt

Pepper

Parsley Flakes

Balsamic Vinegar

Olive Oil

Parmesan Cheese

2 pats of Butter

## Preparation:

In a semi deep, coverable pan, coat ¼ onion chopped, 2 cloves of chopped garlic, 1 diced tomato with olive oil. Add 1 tsp of ground black pepper, ½ tsp of salt, ½ tsp of parsley flakes and stir. Sauté for 1 minute until onions start to become translucent. Add chicken and sauté for 30 additional seconds. Add 2 pats of butter, ¼ cup of balsamic vinegar and stir so that vegetables and chicken are coated and become the darker color of the balsamic. Turn heat to low. Stir and cover to let simmer.

In a separate pot, prepare the pasta according to directions on box. When finished, drain and put into pan with tomatoes, chicken, etc. Stir pasta until coated with balsamic sauce. Add 1 tbsp of olive oil until pasta has been coated. Add 1 tbsp of parmesan cheese, ½ tsp ground pepper and additional parsley if desired. Stir.

### SERVE IT
#### Bit@h!

WORDS OF *Wisdom*
- Balsamic vinegar is a great complement to wheat and flour based foods.
- Chicken takes on a zesty flavor when browned in balsamic vinegar.
- Garlic and pepper complement the flavor of balsamic vinegar.

S&M
*(Sides & More)*
*Appetizer:*
Baked Artichoke
Bruschetta
*Salad:*
Simple tossed salad with choice of homemade dressing.

# CHICKEN WITH *Fungus*
## *(Chicken Marsala with Mushrooms)*

RATING: ARE YOU F%@KING KIDDING *Me?*

*Grocery List:*
Parmesan Cheese
Flour
Garlic Powder
Onion Powder
Parsley Flakes
Salt
Ground Black Pepper
1 Egg
Chicken (2-4 breasts)
Olive Oil
½ Onion chopped
1 clove Garlic sliced
Marsala Wine
1 cup of chopped Mushrooms
Butter
1 can of Chicken Broth

## Preparation:

Mix ½ cup flour with 2 tbsp parmesan cheese, 1 tbsp garlic powder, 1 tbsp onion powder, 1 tbsp parsley flakes, ½ tsp of pepper and a pinch of salt. Crack 1 egg in separate bowl and beat with 1 tsp parmesan cheese, 1 tsp parsley flakes, ½ tsp pepper and a pinch of salt. Prepare chicken pieces by covering in flour mixture, then egg mixture and then dredging in flour mixture again. Set aside.

In a semi-deep, coverable frying pan, add onion and garlic and sauté with enough olive oil to coat. Add garlic powder, salt and pepper to taste. Sauté for 1 minute. Add enough Marsala Wine to cover bottom of pan. Brown chicken on all sides for 30 seconds to one minute until flour mixture is cooked through and adheres to chicken. Take out and set aside.

S&M
(Sides & More)
Appetizer:
Baked Artichoke
Bruschetta
Salad:
Simple tossed salad with choice of
homemade dressing
Choice of Sides:
Zesty Lemon Garlic Potatoes
Broccoli and Garlic in Lemon Butter

In same pan, add more Marsala Wine to cover the bottom of the pan. Add mushrooms and sauté for 30 seconds to 1 minute. Add chicken broth, ¼ cup Marsala Wine, ¼ stick of butter, 1 tsp of garlic powder, 1 tsp of onion powder, 1 tsp parsley flakes, ½ tsp of pepper, salt to taste. Bring to a boil, then simmer. Add chicken (only when it has stopped boiling, no sooner.) Cover and simmer for 40 minutes.

Take chicken out and set aside. Using the broth/Marsala mixture slowly stir in 2 tbsp of flour to thicken sauce. Stir until fairly smooth, try to get all lumps out.

**DISH OUT SAUCE OVER CHICKEN MAKING SURE TO INCLUDE MUSHROOMS AND ONIONS, AND SERVE IT** *Bit@h!*

WORDS OF *Wisdom*

- Simmering meat tends to moisten it.
- Flour can thicken any left over meat "juice" to become a gravy. Adding butter enhances the flavor, as well as the calories.
- Wine adds great flavor to meats when browned in them.
- Battering and breading meats not only adds flavor, but helps to keep the meat moist.
- Putting flavor into the breading enhances the taste. Spice is not only for the meat and the sauce.

# TRAILER PARK CHICKEN *Marsala*

## *(Chicken Marsala Pasta with Mushrooms and Broccoli)*

RATING: **THE LITTLE CHEF THAT** *Could*

*Grocery List:*

Olive Oil
½ Onion chopped
1 clove Garlic sliced
1-2 Chicken Breasts cubed
Marsala Wine
1 cup of chopped Mushrooms
1 can of Chicken Broth
Butter
½ cup of chopped Broccoli
Garlic Powder
Onion Powder
Parsley Flakes
Salt
Ground Black Pepper

Parmesan Cheese
Rigatoni or Penne
Flour

## Preparation:

In a semi-deep, coverable frying pan, add onion and garlic and sauté with enough olive oil to coat. Add salt and pepper to taste. Sauté for 1 minute. Add enough Marsala Wine to cover bottom of pan. Brown cubes of chicken and mushrooms for 30 seconds to one minute.

In same pan, add chicken broth, ¼ cup Marsala Wine, ¼-½ stick of butter, 1 tbsp of garlic powder, 1 tbsp of onion powder, 1 tbsp parsley flakes, ½ tsp of pepper, salt to taste. Bring to a boil, then simmer. Add pasta and broccoli and stir to prevent sticking. Cover and let simmer until pasta is tender (about 10-15 minutes). Add parmesan cheese and stir in 1 tsp of flour to thicken sauce. Stir until thoroughly mixed and most of the lumps are smooth.

### SERVE IT
*Bit@h!*

S&M
(Sides & More)
Appetizer:
Baked Artichoke
Bruschetta
Salad:
Simple tossed salad with choice of homemade dressing

WORDS OF Wisdom
• Dishes with great flavors and sauces will make a great pasta version. (i.e. Chicken Marsala)
• Vegetables can be a great addition to pasta.
• Broccoli can complement darker sauces with a richer flavor well.

# BEGG *Me!*
## *(Curry and Vegetable Egg Bake)*

RATING: **DUMB** *Ass!*

Can be used as a side dish as well.

*Grocery List:*
3 Eggs
½ cup of Broccoli chopped
½ Onion
2 cloves chopped Garlic (larger chunks)
1 Potato diced
½ Lemon
½ cup frozen Peas
½ cup frozen Spinach
½ cup frozen Corn
Salt
Ground Black Pepper
Curry Powder
Chili Powder
Parmesan Cheese

## Preparation:

In a bowl, beat 3 eggs.  Add ½ tbsp of pepper, 1 tbsp of curry powder, ½ tbsp of chili powder, juice of ½ lemon, and ¼ cup of parmesan cheese. Mix thoroughly. Add the rest of the ingredients and stir thoroughly so the vegetables are dispersed throughout egg mixture. Grease a small baking pan. Pour mixture in.

Preheat oven to 325 degrees. Place baking pan with ingredients in the oven and bake for 45 minutes.

### SLICE INTO RECTANGLES AND SERVE IT
*Bit@h!*

S&M
(Sides & More)
Appetizer:
Baked Artichoke
Bruschetta
Salad:
Simple tossed salad with choice of
homemade dressing

# EAT ME! *Eggplant*

## *(Eggplant, Tomatoes and Onions in a Spicy Asian Sauce)*

RATING: **DUMB** *Ass!*

*Grocery List:*

1 small Eggplant sliced
Flour
Ground Black Pepper
Red Wine Vinegar
Soy Sauce
Brown Sugar
Hot Pepper Sauce
Chili Powder
Curry Powder
1 Tomato cut into large chunks
1 Onion sliced the long way
1 clove Garlic sliced or chopped

## Preparation:

Lightly flour the eggplant slices by dipping them in the flour and set aside.

To make the sauce combine ¼ cup of red wine vinegar, ¼ cup of soy sauce, 3 tsp of hot pepper sauce, ½ tsp black pepper, ½ tsp of curry powder, ½ tsp of chili powder, 1 tsp of brown sugar. Mix thoroughly. Set aside.

In a bowl, combine ¾ of the sliced onion (leave a quarter for later) and tomato chunks and lightly coat with olive oil. Set aside.

In a pan, sauté ¼ of sliced onion (that you didn't use above) and chopped garlic with enough olive oil to coat. Brown the eggplant. Then take out and set aside. Add additional onions and tomatoes and sauté for 1 minute. Pour sauce into pan and add up to ¼ cup of water. Bring to a boil. Then lower heat to simmer. Add eggplant and simmer for an additional 30 minutes until eggplant is soft.

**SERVE THOSE VEGGIES**
*Bit@h!*

S&M
*(Sides & More)*
*Appetizer:*
Baked Artichoke
Bruschetta
*Salad:*
Asian Cucumber Salad
Simple tossed salad with choice of
homemade dressing

# GET IN THE KITCHEN, Bit@h!

## Appetizers

I have never been one for appetizers, but I figured since I was writing a cookbook, I should include a few. So here are a *few*.

### BAKED ARTICHOKE

1 fresh Artichoke
1 Lemon
2 pats of Butter
2 tbsp Olive Oil
Garlic Powder
Onion Powder
Ground Black Pepper
Salt
Bread Crumbs

Boil water in a pot big enough to fit the artichoke. Cut the stem (if any) off of the artichoke and place in boiling water. Boil for 20 minutes. Place artichoke on a baking sheet. Squeeze ½ lemon over artichoke. Sprinkle with garlic powder, salt, pepper, onion powder. Preheat oven to 375 degrees. In a sauce pan, melt two pats of butter with pinch of garlic powder, onion powder, ground black pepper, and salt. Add 2 tbsp olive oil as butter melts and stir. When butter melts, squeeze ½ lemon into sauce pan and stir for about 30 seconds. Take off of heat and drizzle over artichoke making sure to cover a bit on each leaf. Sprinkle bread crumbs over artichoke so that they stick to the inside of the leaves. Bake in oven for 15-25 minutes until bread crumbs brown.

**MAKE SURE TO PUT A BOWL OUT FOR THE EATEN LEAVES AND SERVE THE DAMN THING, *Bit@h!***

## BRUSCHETTA

5 Roma (Plum) Tomatoes or 2 large regular Tomatoes
½ Onion chopped
3 sprigs fresh Parsley
Olive Oil
Garlic Powder
Red Wine Vinegar
Balsamic Vinegar
Ground Black Pepper
Salt
Grated Parmesan Cheese
French or Italian Bread

Finely chop tomatoes and place in a bowl. Chop a ½ of an onion finely and add to bowl. Chop 3 sprigs of parsley and add to bowl. Add 5 tbsp of olive oil, 5 tbsp of red wine vinegar, and 2 tbsp of balsamic vinegar. Add 1 tsp of pepper, ½ tsp of salt, 1 tsp of garlic powder, and 1 tbsp of parmesan cheese. Mix thoroughly and refrigerate for an hour.

Slice bread into pieces and arrange on a baking sheet. Sprinkle with parmesan cheese, garlic powder, and ground black pepper. Put in oven at 300 degrees until toasted.

Serve the bread on a platter. The bruschetta can be served in the bowl so your friends and family can dish it out themselves.

**DON'T BE A DUMBASS AND PUT THE BRUSCHETTA MIX ON THE BREAD BEFORE YOU SERVE IT. THIS WILL MAKE IT SOGGY AND YOU WILL LOOK LIKE AN IDIOT.** *Don't be an idiot!*

## SALAMI WRAPS WITH A BALSAMIC DIPPING *Sauce*

Salami
Provolone Cheese
Balsamic Vinegar
Horseradish Mustard
Parsley Flakes
Ground Black Pepper
Roasted Red Peppers in a jar
Toothpicks

Slice salami and provolone into strips and place on top of each other. Roll into a tube and put a toothpick through the top and bottom. Cut a roasted red pepper into little strips and slide down the toothpick until it touches the wrap.

DIPPING Sauce
Combine ½ cup of balsamic vinegar with ¼ cup horseradish mustard, 1 tsp of parsley flakes and ½ tsp of ground black pepper. Mix thoroughly.

**MAKE AS MUCH AS YOUR COMPANY CALLS FOR,**
*Bit@h!*

# GET IN THE KITCHEN,
## *Bit@h!*

## Sides

---

### ZESTY LEMON GARLIC *Potatoes*

2 large Red Potatoes
1 clove Garlic sliced
¼ Onion chopped
Butter
Olive Oil
½ Lemon
Parsley Flakes
Ground Black Pepper
Salt
Parmesan Cheese

Cut potatoes into mouth sized pieces (larger than bite-sized where it takes two bites to eat a piece) and put into a bowl. Squeeze the juice of ½ lemon on top and mix thoroughly.

Melt 3 pats of butter in microwave or on stove, and pour on top of potatoes. Add garlic and onion, salt and pepper to taste, sprinkle of parsley flakes, and 1 tsp of olive oil. Mix thoroughly. Place on baking sheet. Sprinkle parmesan cheese on top. Preheat oven to 350 degrees and bake for 45 minutes (longer if more crisp is desired) until potatoes are tender, yet crisp.

### DISH OUT AND PUT NEXT TO YOUR MAIN COURSE, *Bit@h!*

---

## VEGGIE MASHED *Potatoes*

2 baking Potatoes
2 pats of Butter
Light Sour Cream
¼ cup fresh Baby Carrots
¼ cup frozen Broccoli
¼ cup frozen Peas
Salt
Ground Black Pepper
Garlic Powder
Onion Powder

Cut potatoes in quarters and place with ¼ cup of carrots in a pot of boiling water until tender to the fork (20 minutes or so).

Place in a bowl while still piping hot with a pat of butter, ¼ cup light sour cream, ¼ cup of broccoli, ¼ cup of frozen peas, ½ tsp of pepper, 1 tsp garlic powder, 1 tsp onion powder, and salt to taste. Mash together with masher or back of fork and mix thoroughly.

### PLACE NEXT TO YOUR ENTRÉE,
*Bit@h!*

# CURRY CINNAMON MASHED SWEET *Potatoes*

2 Sweet Potatoes
1 baking Potato
Butter
Cinnamon
Curry Powder
Chili Powder
Garlic Powder
Salt
Ground Black Pepper
Milk

Cut sweet potatoes and regular baking potato in quarters and place in a pot of boiling water until tender to the fork (20 minutes or so).

Place in a bowl while still piping hot with 2 pats of butter, ¼ cup milk, 1 tbsp curry powder, 1 tsp cinnamon, ½ tsp of chili powder, ½ tsp pepper, 1 tsp garlic powder, salt to taste. Mash with masher or back of a fork and mix thoroughly. Mash it until the desired texture. Some may like it more chunky.

### PLACE NEXT TO YOUR ENTRÉE,
*Bit@h!*

# Kugels:

Potato Kugel is a traditional Jewish dish served at holiday gatherings. Below are three original versions of kugels that I think you can enjoy year round. It is basically a potato cake. Don't be skeptical. Live a little you sheltered pig!

## POTATO, BROCCOLI AND CHEESE Kugel

2 Potatoes peeled
1 cup frozen Broccoli
2 slices American Cheese
1 Onion
2 cloves Garlic
2 Eggs
3 heaping tbsp Flour
Ground Black Pepper
Salt
Olive Oil

Cut potatoes into quarters and put in a food processor. Add 1 cup of frozen broccoli, semi thawed, chopped onion, chopped (in half) garlic, cheese, eggs, flour, 1 tsp pepper, 1 tbsp salt and 4 tbsp of olive oil. Blend together until smooth.

In a pre-greased tinfoil cake pan, pour mixture. Cook for 45 minutes to an hour at 350 degrees until center is firm.

### CUT INTO RECTANGLES AND PLACE NEXT TO YOUR ENTRÉE, Bit@h!

## SWEET POTATO *Kugel*

1 Sweet Potato peeled
1 Baking Potato peeled
1 cup Baby Carrots
1 Onion
2 cloves Garlic
2 Eggs
3 heaping tbsp Flour
Cinnamon
Ground Black Pepper
Salt
Olive Oil

Cut potatoes and sweet potatoes into quarters and put in a food processor. Add carrot, chopped onion, chopped garlic, eggs, flour, 1 tsp pepper, 1 tsp of cinnamon, 1 tbsp salt and 4 tbsp of olive oil. Blend together until smooth.

In a pre-greased tinfoil cake pan, pour mixture. Cook for 45 minutes to an hour at 350 degrees until center is firm.

CUT INTO RECTANGLES AND PLACE NEXT TO
YOUR ENTRÉE, *Bit@h!*

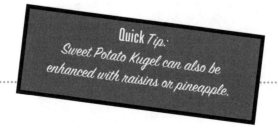

Quick *Tip:*
Sweet Potato Kugel can also be
enhanced with raisins or pineapple.

# VEGETABLE *Kugel*

1 Baking Potato peeled
¼ cup Baby Carrots
1 Onion
¼ cup of Broccoli
¼ cup frozen Spinach
2 cloves Garlic
2 Eggs
3 heaping tbsp Flour
Ground Black Pepper
Salt
Olive Oil

Cut potato into quarters and put in a food processor. Add carrot, chopped onion, chopped garlic, broccoli, spinach, eggs, flour, 1 tsp pepper, 1 tbsp salt and 4 tbsp of olive oil. Blend together until smooth.

In a pre-greased tinfoil cake pan, pour mixture. Cook for 45 minutes to an hour at 350 degrees until center is firm.

CUT INTO RECTANGLES AND PLACE NEXT TO
YOUR ENTRÉE, *Bit@h!*

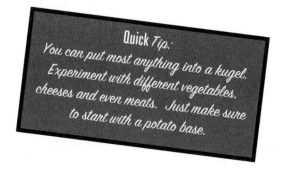

Quick *Tip:*
You can put most anything into a kugel. Experiment with different vegetables, cheeses and even meats. Just make sure to start with a potato base.

# BROCCOLI AND GARLIC IN LEMON *Butter*

Olive Oil
3 cloves of Garlic sliced
3 cups of Broccoli
2 pats of Butter
Ground Black Pepper
Salt
Lemon

In a coverable frying pan place the sliced garlic with enough olive oil to coat and sauté for a minute. Add one pat of butter and broccoli. Squeeze juice of ½ lemon and stir. Add the other pat of butter and mix. Cover and cook until broccoli becomes semi tender and bright green (approximately 5-10 minutes). Salt and pepper to taste.

## PLACE NEXT TO YOUR ENTRÉE,
*Bit@h!*

● ● ● ● ●

# GET IN THE KITCHEN, *Bit@h!*

## Meal and Luncheon Salads

Ever need a quick and easy recipe for a potluck luncheon, barbecue, or picnic? Well, now you have no excuse not to bring a dish that will make your friends beg to be bent over and paddled. Don't be the one to show up empty handed. Everyone hates a cheap, lazy, bit@h!

### PIZZA *Salad*

Mozzarella Cheese
Thin Pizza Crust
Tomato Sauce
1 clove of Garlic chopped
Lettuce
Onions
Carrots
Tomatoes
Olive Oil
Red Wine Vinegar
Roasted Chicken (optional)

Prepare a pizza by using the pizza crust, tomato sauce, mozzarella cheese and chopped garlic. Add ground pepper to taste. Bake for ten minutes or until ready. Set aside to cool.

78

While pizza is cooking, prepare a salad to your liking using vegetables listed. Don't make me tell you how to create a salad... do something for yourself damn it.

Cut pizza into bite sized pieces. Sprinkle, warm, not hot, pizza on the salad. Add 4 tbsp of red wine vinegar, 2 tbsp olive oil, salt, pepper, garlic powder, parsley flakes. Mix thoroughly.

### SERVE IT,
*Bit@h!*

## ASIAN CUCUMBER *Salad*

1 Cucumber sliced thinly
¼ Onion sliced
½ Tomato diced
3 tbsp Soy Sauce
4 tbsp Rice Vinegar
Garlic Powder
Ground Black Pepper

Slice the cucumber into thin discs. If it is thicker than a nickel, you have sliced it too thick. Put them in a bowl and set aside. Slice the onion in long and semi thick pieces and mix into the bowl with the cucumber. Dice the tomato and add as well. Add 3 tbsp of soy sauce, and 4 tbsp of rice vinegar. Add 1 tsp of garlic powder and ½ tsp of pepper.

### MIX THOROUGHLY AND
### SERVE IT, *Bit@h!*

# TUNA RAMEN PASTA *Salad*

1 can of Tuna
¼ Onion chopped
¼ cup frozen Corn (thawed)
2 Pickles chopped finely
¼ cup Carrot
Garlic Powder
Salt
Ground Black Pepper
2 heaping tbsp Mayonnaise
2 tbsp Red Wine Vinegar
1 heaping tbsp Horseradish Mustard
Packet of Ramen Noodles

Cut carrot diagonally and boil until slightly tender. About 10 minutes. Combine onion pickle and carrot in a bowl. Add can of tuna, corn, crushed ramen noodles into the same bowl. Add 1 tsp of garlic powder, ½ tsp of ground black pepper, 1 tsp of onion powder and 1 tsp of salt. Mix thoroughly so that the vegetables and tuna are coated with spices. In same bowl, add 2 heaping tbsp of mayonnaise, 2 tbsp of red wine vinegar, 1 heaping tbsp of horseradish mustard and mix thoroughly. Refrigerate for 25 minutes until ramen noodles are tender.

### EAT THAT TUNA,
*Bit@h!*

# CHICKEN, RICE AND ARTICHOKE *Salad*

½ lb cooked Chicken
2 cups of cooked Rice
½ can of Artichoke Hearts
2 tbsp of Mayonnaise
2 tbsp of Horseradish or Dijon Mustard
2 tbsp of Red Wine Vinegar
1 tsp of Ground Black Pepper
Salt to taste
1 tsp of Garlic Powder
1 tsp of Onion Powder

COMBINE ABOVE INGREDIENTS IN A BOWL THOROUGHLY
AND SERVE IT, *Bit@h!*

# MEDITERRANEAN TUNA *Salad*

1 can of Tuna
1/8 cup of chopped Artichoke Hearts
1/8 cup chopped Black Olives
1/8 cup chopped Red Onion
2 tbsp Mayonnaise
1 tbsp Vinegar
1 tsp Ground Black Pepper
1 tsp Garlic Powder
1 tsp Horseradish or Dijon Mustard
Salt to taste

PLACE ALL INGREDIENTS IN A BOWL AND MIX THOROUGHLY.
GREAT FOR A SANDWICH *Bit@h!*

# HOMEMADE POTATO *Salad*

2-3 medium Potatoes
¼ Onion chopped
2 Eggs
2 Celery stalks chopped
2 chopped Pickles
½ cup Mayonnaise
¼ cup Red Wine Vinegar
¼ cup Horseradish Mustard
1 tsp Ground Black Pepper
1 tbsp Garlic Powder
Salt

Place 2-3 quartered potatoes and 2 whole eggs in a pot. Cover with water and bring to a boil. Eggs will rupture if you put them directly into boiling water. Boil eggs for 10 minutes, and take out of water. Boil potatoes until you can drive a fork in them. Allow to cool.

In a large bowl combine ¼ chopped onion, 2 chopped celery stalks, two chopped pickles, 5 tbsp of red wine vinegar, ½ cup of mayonnaise, ¼ cup of horseradish mustard, 1 tsp of garlic powder, ½ tsp of ground black pepper, cooled potatoes, cooled, peeled eggs. Using a large fork, chop potatoes and eggs into bite-sized chunks. Then mix thoroughly making sure chunks of potato are in tact and not mashed. Salt to taste.

### DO I HAVE TO TELL YOU WHAT TO DO WITH IT?
### JUST EAT THE DAMN THING, *Bit@h!*

● ● ● ● ●                    ● ● ● ● ●

# GET IN THE KITCHEN,
## Bit@h!

## Soups & Stews

Soups and stews can be great for a meal. You don't believe me, bitch?  Well get your ass into the kitchen and try these.

### CRISPY ASIAN CHICKEN *Soup*

2 Chicken Breasts sliced
1 Onion sliced long
2 cloves Garlic
Spaghetti or Linguine
¼ cup Bok Choy
¼ cup Broccoli
¼ cup frozen Corn
1 Egg
¼ cup Flour
Breadcrumbs
Ground Black Pepper
Parsley Flakes
Soy Sauce
Red Wine or Rice Vinegar
Chicken Broth

Mix ¼ cup of flour with ½ tsp ground black pepper, 1 tbsp garlic powder, ¼ cup breadcrumbs. Set aside.

Beat one egg with pinch of pepper and a pinch of parsley flakes. Dip chicken strips into flour mix then egg mix and then dredge in flour again. Set aside.

In a frying pan, sauté ¼ onion sliced and ½ clove chopped garlic with enough olive oil to coat. Add pepper and sauté for 30 seconds. Add 1 tbsp of soy sauce and 1 tbsp of vinegar and mix. Brown chicken strips on all sides until they are crispy, but do not burn (probably for 1-2 minutes, but watch carefully). Take out and set aside. Save onion and garlic for later.

In a large pot, sauté the rest of the sliced onion and chopped garlic in enough olive oil to coat. Add 1 tbsp of vinegar and cook for 30 seconds to a minute. Add can of chicken broth, 1 cup of water, 4 tbsp of soy sauce, 5 tbsp of vinegar, and 1 tsp of pepper. Bring to a boil. Then simmer. When it is simmering, not before, add broccoli, bok choy, and corn. Also add the onions and garlic from browning the chicken. Simmer for 20 minutes.

While soup is simmering: In a separate pot, bring water to a boil to cook pasta. Cook pasta halfway. Drain and put into soup until tender.

**LADLE AND PLACE CHICKEN STRIPS ON TOP. WHAT ARE YOU WAITING FOR? SERVE IT *Bit@h!***

# CHICKEN *Chili*

Olive Oil
2 cloves Garlic chopped
¼ Onion chopped
1 lb Ground Chicken
1 can of Red Beans
1 can of diced Tomatoes
½ cup frozen Corn
¼ cup Red Wine Vinegar
Chili Powder
Onion Powder
Garlic Powder
Paprika
Cumin
Oregano
1 can Tomato Paste
Hot Pepper Sauce
Ground Black Pepper
Salt
Parmesan Cheese

In a large pot, sauté garlic and onions in two tablespoons of olive oil for one minute. Add ground meat and brown. Lower heat and add tomatoes and beans. Add ¼ cup of vinegar, 3 tbsp of chili powder, 2 tbsp of garlic powder, 2 tbsp of onion powder, 1 tbsp of salt, 1 tsp of ground black pepper, 1 tsp cumin, 1 tsp paprika, 1 tsp oregano, tomato paste, 2 tbsp of hot pepper sauce, ½ cup of frozen corn, ¼ cup of parmesan cheese. Stir until evenly mixed. Let simmer for three hours stirring occasionally.

SERVE IT *Bit@h!*

## SHERRY DRENCHED BEEF *Stew*

1 clove Garlic chopped
½ Onion chopped
1 Potato diced
Olive Oil
Ground Black Pepper
Salt
½ lb cubed Beef
2 Carrots diced
¼ cup chopped Broccoli
¼ cup of frozen Peas
Sherry Wine
Worcestershire Sauce
¼ stick of Butter
1 can of Beef Broth
2 tbsp of Flour

In a medium to large pot, sauté garlic, onion and potatoes in olive oil. Add pepper and a pinch of salt. Stir frequently. Sauté a minute to two minutes. Add ¼ cup of Sherry wine and stir. Add beef and brown, stirring frequently. Let sauté until beef is lightly browned. Add beef broth, butter, 1 tbsp of Worcestershire Sauce and ¼ cup more of Sherry wine. Add ½ tsp of pepper and pinch of salt. Stir and bring to a boil. Let boil for less than a minute and simmer. Add broccoli and carrots. Simmer for 20-30 minutes. Mix in flour stirring so that all lumps are removed. Let simmer for another 10-15 minutes.

### SERVE IT UP
*Bit@h!*

# GET IN THE KITCHEN, *Bit@h!*

## Homemade Salad Dressings

Making homemade salad dressing is fun. Well, not as fun as masturbating, but still a great time. I'm not talking about those that come from a packet, I am talking about the ones that you make from scratch. This way, you know exactly what's going into them. They are healthy and they are delicious! Try a few of these, bitch!

### HOMEMADE *Italian*

½ cup Red Wine Vinegar
¼ cup Olive Oil
1 tbsp Garlic Powder
½ tsp Ground Black Pepper
½ tsp Salt
1 tbsp Onion Powder
1 tbsp Parmesan Cheese
1 tbsp Parsley Flakes

**THOROUGHLY MIX IT TOGETHER IN A BOWL**
*Bit@h!*

## HOMEMADE RUSSIAN OR THOUSAND *Island*

Mayonnaise
Vinegar
Ketchup
Finely diced pickle
Garlic Powder
Onion Powder
Ground Black Pepper
Paprika

Combine ½ cup of mayonnaise with 3 tbsp of vinegar, 4 tbsp ketchup, 1 finely diced pickle, 1 tsp each of garlic powder and onion powder, ½ tsp each of ground black pepper and paprika. Mix thoroughly.

### DRIZZLE IT ON YOUR SALAD,
*Bit@h!*

## HORSERADISH-MUSTARD *Vinaigrette*

Horseradish Mustard
Vinegar
Olive Oil
Garlic Powder
Ground Black Pepper
Parsley Flakes
Onion Powder

Combine ¼ cup of horseradish mustard with ½ cup of red wine vinegar, 2 tbsp of olive oil, ½ tsp garlic powder, ½ tsp onion powder, pinch of ground black pepper, ½ tsp of parsley flakes. Mix thoroughly.

### DRIZZLE IT ON YOUR SALAD,
*Bit@h!*

## SIMPLY *Balsamic*

Balsamic Vinegar
Red Wine Vinegar
Olive Oil
Garlic Powder
Onion Powder
Parsley Flakes
Ground Black Pepper
Salt
Parmesan Cheese

Combine ¼ cup of balsamic vinegar with 2 tbsp of red wine vinegar, ¼ cup olive oil, 1 tsp garlic powder, 1 tsp onion powder, 1 tsp parsley flakes, ½ tsp ground black pepper, pinch of salt and 1 tbsp of parmesan cheese. Mix thoroughly.

### DRIZZLE IT ON YOUR SALAD,
*Bit@h!*

## CREAMY *Italian*

½ cup Mayonnaise
¼ cup of Red Wine Vinegar
1 tbsp of Olive Oil
½ tsp of Salt
½ tsp of Ground Black Pepper
1 tsp of Garlic Powder
1 tsp of Onion Powder
1 tsp of Parsley Flakes
1 tsp of Parmesan Cheese

### I'M NOT EVEN GOING TO WASTE MY TYPING ON YOU.
### MIX IT TOGETHER FOR PETE *Sake!*

## HONEY *Balsamic*

¼ cup  Balsamic Vinegar
4 tbsp  Honey
1 tbsp  Garlic Powder
½ tbsp  Ground Black Pepper
½ tsp  Salt
¼ cup  Olive Oil

**JEEZ! JUST MIX THE ABOVE INGREDIENTS TOGETHER THOROUGHLY. DON'T YOU GET IT BY NOW,** *Bit@h?*

## CRANBERRY *Balsamic*

½ cup  Balsamic Vinegar
¼ can of whole  Cranberry Sauce
1 tbsp  Garlic Powder
½ tbsp  Pepper
½ tsp  Salt
¼ cup  Olive Oil

**YOU KNOW WHAT TO DO. MIX IT TOGETHER THOROUGHLY** *Bit@h!*

● ● ● ● ● ● ●

# SO, TOO DAMN LAZY TO START FROM SCRATCH, *Huh?*

Well, well, well...aren't you the lazy bitch. You just can't take it upon yourself to start a dish from scratch, huh? Well...I knew there were some of you out there. So, I put together a couple of tips for those nights when you just don't feel like doing it all. Fortunately, there are some great packaged food products on the market that can help you create meals that are fast, cheap, and most importantly, good.

## FROZEN *Pizza*

You can make frozen pizza into an incredible meal. All you have to do is add some fresh or frozen vegetables, meat, and spice it up with garlic powder, pepper, onion powder, and bake. I like to put some red wine vinegar or barbecue sauce on mine after it has been cooked to add a bit more zest...but as you know, I may be a freak. Try it! You may be a silly freak also.

# SOUPS

It's so easy to make a homemade meal out of a can of soup. All you need to do is add more stuff!

## Chicken or Beef Based Soups

Start out with a can of chicken or beef broth based soups. Examples include Chicken Noodle, Beef and Vegetables, Chicken and Rice, etc. Just make sure you do not use a cream-based soup like Clam Chowder. I'll talk about those later...hold your damn horses.

The object is to create a soup that is substantial and flavorful. If you simply add water, then you will have a watered down mess. So, start out by pouring the soup into a pot (I find that pots work better than pouring it directly onto your stove). Add a can of water. Yes, even to the ones that say don't add a can of water...live on the wild side. As this will dilute the taste of the soup, you will have to add more flavor. Tangy flavors such as lemon or vinegar really complement the salty taste of canned soup well. Also, by not adding more salt, the sodium level will be lower. Here are a couple of recipes for chicken and beef based soups that you may enjoy. You also may not enjoy them, and in that case, I don't really give a sh*t. I like em', and that's really all that matters.

# ASIAN CHICKEN OR BEEF *Soup-*
## TRIPLE DUMB-*Ass*

Olive Oil
¼ Onion chopped
Can of Chicken or Beef Broth-based soup
¼ cup frozen Corn
¼ cup Broccoli
Soy Sauce
Red Wine Vinegar or Balsamic Vinegar
Curry Powder
Chili Powder
Ground Black Pepper
Chicken Breast or Beef cubed
Pasta

In a pot, sauté onion with enough olive oil to coat. Slice chicken breast or beef into small cubes and sauté with onions for an additional half minute until it starts to brown. Then add two swigs of soy sauce, two swigs of vinegar, sprinkling of curry and chili powder and sauté a bit longer so that the vegetable and chicken soak up some flavor (about a minute more.) Add can of soup and one can of water. Add 1 tbsp of soy sauce and 3 tbsp of vinegar. Add 1 tsp of curry powder, 1 tsp chili powder and ground black pepper to taste and stir. Bring to a boil for 30 seconds and then lower heat to simmer. Add the rest of the vegetables as well as the pasta. Simmer for 20 minutes. Salt to taste.

SERVE IT...WELL YOU KNOW WHAT YOU ARE BY *Now.*

## CREAM-BASED *Soups*

There are a couple of things that you can do to make cream-based soups taste great and go farther. Putting in milk will add to the base, but again will dilute the flavor and the thickness. In order to replace the thickness, try adding a little flour. I find that a lemon always makes a cream-based soup taste incredible. Hot pepper sauce spices up cream-based soups tremendously as well! Adding vegetables, pasta and meat to cream-based soups will also increase its volume.

Below are recommendations on vegetables and other foodstuffs (damn, I love that word, I really don't get the chance to use it as much as I want to) that you can add to cream-based soups to make it go farther and taste great!

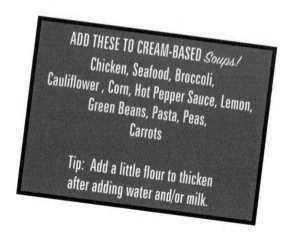

ADD THESE TO CREAM-BASED *Soups!*
Chicken, Seafood, Broccoli, Cauliflower, Corn, Hot Pepper Sauce, Lemon, Green Beans, Pasta, Peas, Carrots

Tip: Add a little flour to thicken after adding water and/or milk.

# PACKAGED *Rice*

Packaged rice isn't just good for a side dish; it can be a great base for a homemade meal. Here are some great recipes for packaged rice. I prefer to use the packaged rice with the flavor packets as opposed to the ones with the flavoring mixed in. This way you can choose how much of the seasoning you want to use. So buy those, damn it!

## *Beef Flavored*

The beef flavor can be a great base for a beef or chicken in a Sherry Wine Sauce.

Beef flavored Rice-a-Foni
1 cup Beef or Chicken cubed
¼ Onion chopped
2 cloves of Garlic chopped or sliced
½ cup Carrots diced or sliced
¼ cup Peas
Sherry Wine
2 pats of Butter
Ground Black Pepper

In a semi-deep frying pan, sauté onions and garlic in enough olive oil to coat the vegetables for about 1 minute. Add cubed chicken or beef, ½ tsp of ground black pepper, and let sauté for about 30 seconds. Add enough Sherry wine to coat the bottom of the pan. Stir the vegetables and meat until browned. Add the rice from the package and  sauté for about 30 seconds. Add an additional ½ cup of Sherry wine, 1½ cups of water, 2 pats of butter, ¼-½ of seasoning and stir. Add carrots and peas. Stir to make sure rice doesn't stick to the bottom of the pan. Cover and bring to a boil. Then simmer until liquid is absorbed into the rice.

*Chicken Flavored*

If you're a smart bitch, you will have noticed there is a great recipe (Curry The F%@k Up!) that uses chicken flavored Rice-a-Foni. It's on page 39, so look it up. I am not going to waste any more time on you by repeating it here.

However, I will give you a really quick and easy recipe for Chicken Fried Rice.

Chicken flavored Rice-a-Foni
1 cup Chicken cubed
¼ Onion chopped
2 cloves of Garlic chopped or sliced
½ cup Carrots diced or sliced
¼ cup Peas
¼ cup frozen corn
¼ cup soy sauce
¼ cup vinegar
1 Egg
Ground Black Pepper

In a semi-deep frying pan, sauté onions and garlic in enough olive oil to coat the vegetables for about 1 minute. Add cubed chicken ½ tsp of ground black pepper, and let sauté for about 30 seconds. Stir the vegetables and meat until browned. Add the rice from the package and sauté for about 30 seconds. Add soy sauce and vine-gar, 1½ cups of water, ¼ of seasoning and stir. Add carrots. Stir to make sure rice doesn't stick to the bottom of the pan. Cover and bring to a boil. Then simmer until liquid is absorbed into the rice. Turn heat up to medium high and add peas and carrots. Add the beaten egg and mix thoroughly until egg is cooked.

*Mushroom Flavored*

The mushroom flavor is a great base for a chicken or beef in a Marsala Wine Sauce. Listen up, bitch. I'm only gonna tell you how to do this once. But I guess you can read it over and over again if you're stupid.

Mushroom Flavored Rice-a-Foni
½ lb Beef or Chicken cubed
¼ Onion chopped
2 cloves of Garlic chopped or sliced
½ cup chopped Broccoli
Marsala Wine
2 pats of Butter
Ground Black Pepper

In a semi-deep frying pan, sauté onions and garlic in enough olive oil to coat the vegetables for about 1 minute. Add cubed chicken or beef, ½ tsp of ground black pepper, and let sauté for about 30 seconds. Add enough Marsala wine to coat the bottom of the pan. Stir the vegetables and meat until browned. Add the rice from the package and sauté for about 30 seconds. Add an additional ½ cup of Marsala wine, 1½ cups of water, 2 pats of butter, ¼-½ of mushroom seasoning and stir. Add broccoli. Stir to make sure rice doesn't stick to the bottom of the pan. Cover and bring to a boil. Then lower heat and simmer until liquid is absorbed into the rice.

NOW WASN'T THAT EASY! I TOLD YA' YOU
COULD COOK, *Bit@h!*

*All Flavors*

If you're even lazier than I was thinking, you might want to just add some extra ingredients to any flavor Rice-a-Foni. All flavors can be made into a meal in minutes. All you need is meat, and some vegetables.

Brown the veggies and meat in some olive oil. Then prepare the rice as indicated on the package in the same pan.

**IT'S THAT DAMN EASY,**

*Bit@h!*

Quick Tip for Any Type of Flavored Rice-A-Foni

*Make a meal in minutes: Just sauté some vegetables and meat in olive oil and prepare the Rice-a-Foni as indicated.*
*Try adding some ground black pepper, garlic powder, vinegar and soy sauce to make it "Asian."*

# LEARNING TO LOVE YOUR
## *Leftovers!*

Ok, bitch. It's time to think creatively. Do you think you can do that? Under no circumstance should you throw out leftovers just because you want something different. There are so many things you can do with leftovers to create new and exciting dishes. You can make soups, pastas, stews, you name it! Spice up your leftovers and create a whole new meal that you will love to eat again. Now, get back in that kitchen! We're not done yet!

## LEFTOVER BEEF OR *Steak*

1. Use steak or beef in soups or stews.
2. Use in stir-fry or cook it up with rice. A great stir-fry sauce consists of a mixture of soy sauce, vinegar with a dash of Worcestershire and hot pepper sauces.

## LEFTOVER *Pizza*

1. Add cold or warm pizza to a freshly made salad and add a vinegar based dressing...YUM!

## LEFTOVER *Chicken*

1. Use chicken in soups or stews.

2. Use in stir-fry or cook it up with rice. A great stir-fry sauce consists of a mixture of soy sauce and vinegar with a dash of Worcestershire and hot pepper sauces.

3. Left over chicken in a non-cream-based Italian sauce of any kind usually works great in salads! Try putting chicken parmagiana in a salad with a vinaigrette dressing. Don't be afraid to experiment.

## LEFTOVER *Tacos*

1. Leftover tacos are great to use in pasta sauces. They make a great meat sauce and all you do is add some more seasonings, vegetables, or tomato sauce.

QUICK TIP FOR LEFTOVERS

Don't worry about what sauces and flavorings your leftovers have. You can change the flavors of your leftovers by adding different sauces. Chicken Marsala can be great in an Asian stir-fry for instance. Just try to keep the flavors complementary and your leftovers will take on a whole new life!

# THERE'S HOPE FOR YOU YET,
## *Bit@h!*

Well, bitch. You've been through a lot. I know I've given you a lot to digest. Get it...digest...ha! I kill me. You've tried out the recipes and made some amazing meals. Congratulations! You aren't the useless piece of trash that you were before we met.

I know I have been quite hard on you...but to tell you the truth, I think you needed to be bitch-slapped a little. It's called "tough love" sweetheart. Deal with it. My hope is that you came away with a better sense of how to cook for yourself and what flavors work well together so that you can make awesome homemade meals on your own. That doesn't mean you shouldn't buy the sequels to this book. You're not that good.

Experiment! Use what you have learned to go out on limbs. Don't be afraid to put a cucumber or a banana where it doesn't belong! You will find that you just might like it. I am proud of you!

# BON APPÉTIT,
## *Bit@hes!*

# RECIPE *Listing*

## Appetizers

## Sides

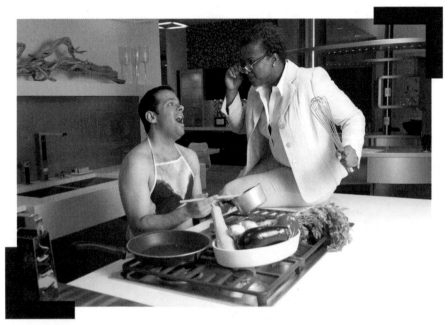

# PHOTO *Gallery*

# PHOTO *Gallery*

# ABOUT THE
## *Author*

Jason Bailin is an amateur chef and professional financier who got tired of the Rat Race, woke up one day and said "SCREW THIS SH*T!" Armed with his spatula and what his mother assured him was a "great idea", he set out to write what has to be the most important literary work of our time, "GET IN THE KITCHEN, Bit@hes!" Frustrated with all of the sweet and cuddly chefs that made him want to smack them in the face with a frying pan, he aimed to write a new kind of cookbook. He's not gonna coddle you, hold your hand or even tell you that you look hot in an apron. He's not your momma, sweet-heart. He's your daddy, bit@h!

# THE *Bit@h's*
## *Notes*

# THINK YOU'VE LEARNED ENOUGH TO CREATE YOUR OWN DAMN RECIPE?

*Write it here, Bit@h!*

# AHH, HOW CUTE. YOU THINK YOU'RE A GOOD COOK.

*Write your recipe here, Bit@h!*